. . . and so it is

Meditations for the Soul

By Michelle Wadleigh

Edited by Suzanne Reeds

Dedication

This book is dedicated to a place in you that matters, to the place in you that has never been hurt, harmed, or injured in any way.

Acknowledgements

Thank you to my sons Michael, Keith, and Seth for standing by me always. Thank you to all my students who make me a better teacher. Thank you to Suzanne Reeds for keeping me honest as I teach Principle. Thank you to Joel Fotinos for his friendship and inspiration. Thank you to all the people who surround me, support me, and believe in my mission—Love. Neil, thank you for showing me what unconditional love looks like. Without all of you, none of this work would be possible. The world is a better place because you are in it. No word of thanks would be complete without the mention of my greatest influence, my teacher, my guide, Rita Sperling.

Read something lovely every day. Read words of love every day. Speak words of love and support every day. Fill your mind and your heart with that which transforms your inner being. Every word spoken and every word read is likened to a brush stroke in a master piece; the masterpiece is you.

Remember who you are

It is time for the world as a whole to remember, to remember its perfection, to remember that we are a product of the Divine Essence of Good that goes by many names. Good exists *everywhere;* it is more abundant than we choose to believe simply because it is so easy to allow our attention to be caught up in the drama, the news, and the complaints of life.

Once we each take on the language of Good, the thoughts of Good, once we begin to seek out the Good in each other, Good will become more abundant, more apparent. I hope that reading the following meditations, affirmations of a sort, will serve to remind you of what your inner wisdom already knows.

It is our time to return to the innocence of our childhood in how we view the world while we act from the place of adults who remember that Good reigns over all.

Please read these meditations in the spirit with which they were intended. To wake up once again to Good, to Love and to remember that We are that Good, that Love

.

*People who love each other fully
and truly are the happiest people
in the world. They may have little,
they may have nothing, but they
are happy people. Everything
depends on how we love one
another.*

~Mother Teresa

*Sometimes you just have
to command LOVE!*

~Michelle Wadleigh

In the beginning was the Word. This Word is empowered with the nonlocal power of this Universe; it is always available, and everywhere present. It is the creative tool of Life.

I use this word wisely and with love, acknowledging that the Word need not always be spoken; the Word creates as much through silent intention as through the spoken declarative word.

The words that I use to create are words that open my heart and mind to be more and more available to Life— Life's influences and Life's inspiration.

My faith grows as I remember that it is my job to make more room for the expression of goodness, and to celebrate all of its forms.

I make room for transformation by being available, and I choose to believe in POSSIBILITY.

Goodness shall have its way with me today because I invite it in fully. This goodness shows up in a multitude of amazing forms; I accept them as the gift that they are.

And so it is.

Don't let yesterday use up too much of today.

~Cherokee Indian Proverb

There is only Now.
This now is relative.
This now can be a nanosecond,
a minute, an hour,
a week, or a lifetime.
Our now is based on a human
invention, ineffective at best.
The Universal now is eternal and
infinite, and cannot be measured
in the same terms.

~Michelle Wadleigh

Today I remember to apply Ancient Wisdom
        to my fullest understanding.
Today I remember to look away from anything
        that would distract me from my good,
        and look to what my heart desires.
Today I think, speak, and act affirmatively all day long.
Today I give of my overflow, and activate the law to prosper me
        now.
I give love when called to.
I act with patience and show compassion.
I speak my truth clearly and act from that clarity.
And I say yes to all of my inspirations as I remember that every
        day is a new opportunity for Good.
Today I dance in the creative process of life and show up in my
        fullness. And, most importantly, I remember that I am
        worthy of a life of beautiful, healthy and prosperous
        expression.
Life is comprised of a simple truth, simple actions, powerful
        results. Today I woke, and the sun was shining, and I was
        breathing on my own, and I was dry, and in my own
        home, and stood on my own two feet to brush my teeth.
Today I got to think on my own, make choices based on my
        desires. I moved around freely without fear.
Today I got to worship freely, laugh at myself,
        and be in awe of life.
Today my life showed me my abundance, my freedom, my
        strength.
I call my life good, lovely and satisfying. Today I celebrate
        Spirit as me, and say "thank you" to that indwelling Spirit
        that breathes life into me each and every day.
        I accept and let it be so.

And so it is.

Peace comes from within.
Do not seek it without.

~Siddhārtha Gautama

Say this often:
There is One Life
This Life is Good
This Life is my life NOW.

~Michelle Wadleigh

There is One life, that life is Spirit's life, that life is Perfect, and
it is my life now.

As I allow myself to be fully absorbed into this One, all
thoughts, habits and behaviors that once were
anchored from a belief in separation are healed.

I guide my subconscious to heal all evidence of separation; this
happens gently and thoroughly. As the false evidence is
healed, my Truth is revealed.

As this healing takes place, I enjoy the fruit of this *changed mind,*
and enjoy how this change has enriched my relationships,
how I now walk fearlessly in the world, how I remember
every day that no one is against me, no one.

This thought alone frees mountains of my energy
to be used creatively.

Yes, today I begin to walk in the ONENESS,
being fully conscious of this truth.

My gratitude runs over and I am blessed.

And so it is.

I never think of the future—
it comes soon enough.

~Albert Einstein

T.G.I.F.
    Thank
    Goodness
    I'm
    Free.
    Free to be me.
    Free to succeed.
    Free to be complete.

~Michelle Wadleigh

Thank Goodness, I'm free.

Yes, thank Goodness, I am a free agent, free to be whom and
what I choose to be, free to choose to follow my heart,
free to heal and to be revealed.

I am grateful for being ordained as a free being, able to access
all good all the time, free to express this good through my
thoughts, words and actions.

May I always use my freedom in a way that lifts others
and celebrates their freedom.

May I be a walking example of what freedom looks like
as love and compassion.

May I be devoted to how spiritual and personal freedom
transforms the world.

Today I celebrate my freedom.

And so it is.

Hatred does not cease by hatred,
but only by love;
this is the eternal rule.

~Siddhārtha Gautama

An abundant dose
Of LOVE
Melts
All resistance.
Heals all distractions.
Reveals all Good.

~Michelle Wadleigh

There is one Life, this life is Good, this life is the always
   present, ever available essence of Good.

There is nothing outside of this experience.

There is no idea contrary to it in any way.

I bask in the Oneness, and the Oneness basks in me.

Within this merging, I become fully absorbed, and as I am
   absorbed by it, I become only It; only Life Beauty.

As the full expression of Life Beauty, all my desires are known
   immediately and acted upon.

I allow Spirit's glorious, spontaneous expression
   to show up through me.

And as it does, it is good, it is loving, and it is complete,
   as I am complete.

No desire is outside the purview of Spirit,
   so I let Spirit express through me.

I call this good, and as I do,

Spirit informs my entire being.

In complete surrender, I express my gratitude by staying
   conscious of my breath.

I let it be so, and so it is!

Let the force be with you.
                         ~Obi-Wan Kenobi

"Let the Force be with you"
was one of the most brilliant
creations of the modern,
pop-culture.
There is a Force for good
and it is here for each to use.
Let's use it wisely.
                         ~Michelle Wadleigh

The Life Force that is everywhere present is the very Life Force
that surges through my body, my mind and my soul. I feel
it intimately, and this assures me of my Oneness with it.

This Life Force is beautiful and masterful with how it shows up
through each individual, and how it evidences itself
through so much good and so much grace.
I recognize Its existence by the fruit that it bears.

And this is good.

I continue my chosen task of waking up and being revealed, and
to support this, I declare that anything and everything that
currently sits anywhere in my subconscious and has
henceforth sabotaged my full, well-rounded expression is
cast out and released.

The vacuum that is created is replaced with an inflow
of good in its unadulterated form.

Yes, I declare that where there was any distraction, there is now
wholeness, fullness, abundance, and love.

All is well in my world.

With great appreciation, I release this word into the
Law of Life with absolute faith.

And so it is!

"One of the great difficulties
in the new order of thought is that
we are likely to indulge
in too much theory
and too little practice."

~Ernest Holmes

I am the change I want to see in
this world, so I step into action.
My action is guided and informed
by the greater Intelligence that
exists.

~Michelle Wadleigh

There is One perfect expression; that expression is Life, that
   Life is perfect, and it is my life now. Wherever I am is the
   full expression of Life. Every step I take and every breath
   that I breathe is a testament to the One.

As I step forward into the fullness of my expression,
   I remember to stay grounded in all moments.
   I remember who I am and what is important to me. The
   consciousness of Spirit fills me so completely that I am
   left wanting for nothing.

There is nothing needed to fill or satisfy me because
   Life is my complete sufficiency.

From my fullness I make all decisions. I am so full, so satisfied,
   that any attempt to feel more complete through old habits
   of materialism are replaced with being fully satiated at all
   times. This happens with ease and grace. I want for
   nothing because I have everything.

There is nothing that could be added to my experience of this
   life that could make it more potent and fulfilling. What is
   expanded through me is my love, my enthusiasm, and my
   sense of celebration.

With gratitude to this indwelling Spirit, I celebrate the One
   while releasing this word into Law.

And so it is!

The gardener goes forth in faith to sow his seeds.

~ Ernest Holmes

Sow your seeds often.
Sow them well.
Sow them deeply, confidently, and in private.
Let no critics see your garden until the harvest,
when they will be in awe!

~ Michelle Wadleigh

Recognizing the All in everything, recognizing the love that
permeates and penetrates all spaces, and recognizing how
this love is the impulsion of the Law; I make myself
available to the experience of the All.

I rest knowing that this Divine Energy is my sufficiency.

Yes, as this Energy makes itself available in every molecule of
my being, I live, work, and experience my being in
knowing that Life is my sufficiency at all times, in all
ways. There is nothing that I yearn for that can satisfy me
more than the fullness of Spirit as my soul is fully
satisfied.

I choose to stay conscious of how Spirit satisfies all needs,
wants, and desires before I even ask.

I enjoy the form, but worship nothing that lives
on the outside of me.

This knowing empowers me to stay present to all good,
all possibility, all the time.

I reach for nothing outside of myself; instead I turn in and
remember I AM the perfect reflection of this Life
impulse.

I live and breathe into gratitude, and watch as it multiplies my
good.

For this beautiful Truth, and so much more, I am eternally
grateful.

And so it is!

Suffering may be salutary in that it leads us to a place where we learn that it is unnecessary! We shall cease to suffer as we more and more comply with the Laws of the Universe. . .

~ Ernest Holmes

Suffering is a distraction from our greatness.
Give up the suffering and make room for the magnificence that you are!

~ Michelle Wadleigh

THERE IS ONLY LIFE, ONLY GOOD, ONLY LIFE
KNOWING ITSELF as me and as all that I see. I accept
this and all my inheritance of good.

Today I lean into the understanding that my life is meant to be
EASY.

Yes, I now place all of my attention on the Truth that suffering
is not only a limiting idea; it is completely incongruent
to my place in life.

I begin to seek out all places in my thinking, my believing, and
my interactions with others that are anchored in any belief
that life is hard, cold, and dissatisfying.

This lie has been perpetrated by years of conditioning, directly
and subliminally, but NO MORE.

These ideas that have lived anywhere in my consciousness are
now cast out and released with love. This happens now
with ease and grace.

So I declare that I am awake and that Life is Good, Life is Easy,
Life is Graceful, and I align with this Truth in everything
that I do and every thought that I have and every decision
that I make.

It is Life's good pleasure to give of Its kingdom, and I
ACCEPT.

I accept all good in all forms, I accept the bountiful blessings as
life with a high expectancy of good.

Accepting and appreciating this truth, I release this word into
Law and into the Awe.

And so it is!

. . . our outlook on life must be transformed by the renewing of the mind, and even when the results are not immediately forthcoming, we must still maintain a calm serenity of thought.

~Ernest Holmes

Transformation does not have to be complicated.
Transformation can be as simple as keeping your eye on the Presence that dwells within.
Our job is to live into the Yes and I accept.
Spirit will do the rest!

~Michelle Wadleigh

There is only an ever-flowing Essence of Good.

There are only expressions of this Good.

I am always right in the middle of this Good; it is my very being.

Anytime that anything distracts me from this truth, I acknowledge it and free myself from its influence by simply saying, "No, thank you."

Simply said, this ever-flowing Essence of Good is my all and my everything, my center, and my circumference. I live, breathe, and act from this Truth, and it is Good.

Life is good—all the time.

With gratitude for all, I celebrate this Life as me.

And so it is!

Principle is not bound by Precedent.

~Thomas Troward

We are never at the mercy of anything—NEVER!

~Michelle Wadleigh

I stand in the knowing that all that I see, all that I experience, and all that appears to be "real" is an effect to a cause that I have set in motion.

If I see it, name it, and experience it, it is within my purview, and is open to a new way of being seen, named, and created.

This movement is not created of the me that I have become, but of the I Am that exists beyond the boundaries of me that has existed for all of time. I am empowered by this knowing because it represents an Intelligence with a reach beyond my local self.

My job is to remember that I can always set a new series of causes and effects in motion by having a change of mind. The love of Spirit is the impulsion that fires this possibility, and it does so in all moments.

Remaining absolutely receptive and staying awake, I now bask in the empowerment that this truth brings.

And so it is.

"Do not ask your children
to strive for extraordinary lives.
Such striving may seem admirable,
but it is the way of foolishness.
Help them instead to find the wonder
and the marvel of an ordinary life.
Show them the joy of tasting
tomatoes, apples and pears.
Show them how to cry
when pets and people die.
Show them the infinite pleasure
in the touch of a hand.
And make the ordinary come alive for them.
The extraordinary will take care of itself."

~William Martin
The Parent's Tao Te Ching,
Ancient Advice for Modern Parents

Do not attempt to be extraordinary;
that shows arrogance.
Be absolutely ordinary and live life in
an extraordinary way.

~Michelle Wadleigh

Oh Mother, Father, Spirit, allow me on this day to recognize the possibility of success, healing, and love that exists right in the midst of everything around me.

Let me have the point of view that never gets distracted by what I see.

Instead of seeing an individual as angry, let me see him as longing for love. Instead of seeing incompetence, let me see that individual as lifting himself out of adversity and doing the best he can.

Instead of taking offense, let me breathe through the tough moments, and not take anything personally.

Let me walk the walk of the mystic, of the wise. Let me *be* love, let me *be* the healing in the room.

I make room for this way of being, and open myself to all of Life's influence and guidance. For this grace, and so much more, I give my thanks, and release this word into Universal Law and to love.

And so it is.

*Love is the central flame of the
universe, nay,
the very fire itself.*

~ Ernest Holmes

*LOVE
IS
FIERCE!*

~Michelle Wadleigh

I speak my word and trust that it is heard, received, and acted upon. This happens with ease because the Infinite Invisible must act; it must create, because its very nature is to create.

Trusting this Infinite Invisible to activate itself through my word, I take great care to provide a word that is focused on the most positive outcome possible.

I mind my word with great care, and I always remember to focus on building a field of consciousness that sets the foundation for good; good that is expected and unexpected.

Each day, I become more practiced as to how I use my word, and I am always more responsible and more focused, not on results, but on my oneness with Spirit, and how I allow Spirit's full expression through me.

This happens with ease and grace each and every day.

Accepting this as so, I express my gratitude by being thankful for all aspects of my life all the time.

And so it is.

*"When you judge another,
you do not define them,
you define yourself."*

~ Wayne Dyer

*There
Is
Only
One.
One love,
One heart,
One intelligence,
which we all access,
One relationship grounded in the
pure genius of this Life.*
~Michelle Wadleigh

Today I live in the knowing that I have one relationship. This relationship fills and satisfies my soul, and I never want or need for anything because I am fully satiated.

Spirit's blanket of love protects and surrounds me always. Everywhere I go, even if the place is new to me, it feels familiar and safe because of this blanket. I know I am cared for. I am always guided, guarded and protected.

This relationship in the One is sweet and simple, and I am consistently invited to walk in and act from my faith that the One infiltrates my being and activates all good through me.

I love how this One continues to show up in my life, in places expected and unexpected, and in infinite ways. Spirit is so awe-inspiring it takes my breath away.

With gratitude for this abundance, I continue to walk in faith, fully expressing my gratitude each moment that I can. I am so grateful, and release this word into this Awesome Law.

And so it is.

Limitation is not in Principle nor in Law, but only in the individual use
we make of Principle.

~Ernest Holmes

Anything that anyone can do ANYONE can do!
Do it NOW!
It's your only time.

~Michelle Wadleigh

There is One intelligence; this one intelligence is known everywhere simultaneously. This One is Good. This One is whom I am when I recognize it and when I don't; never separate, never outside, always only the One.

Each day in my spiritual practices, I focus my attention on welcoming the full realization of this One. I spend more time each and every day in the practice of surrender. Each day I look inside more and outside less, each day I trust more that my life is the very life of Spirit, and I always go directly to the one Source, one Inspiration, One essence of Good and greater Good.

There are no outside rewards that fill me more than I am filled with the realization that I am one with the One. Spirit fills and satisfies all my needs, all my wants, and all my desires, even before they are spoken. My relationship with the One is constantly becoming more and more sophisticated and satisfying. I am no longer distracted by my stories or conditioning.

As I embrace this truth, the texture of my life looks and feels different; it is lovelier, more inviting, and always safer. I am so blessed to know this truth as much as I do. I am fed at all levels, and grateful for the eternal and infinite nature of Goodness that surrounds and infiltrates my being now.

Feeling blessed, I release this word to the Law.

And so it is.

*Your faith can penetrate clouds of
unbelief and reveal the Truth,
which is forever perfect.
Your words do not create this
Truth they merely reveal It.*

~Ernest Holmes
This Thing Called You

*Our job is to cultivate faith.
Not blind or uninformed faith.,
but the faith that is gleaned by
practice, by study, and by proving
that Life Most Definitely is
Working
in Your Favor.*

~Michelle Wadleigh

Knowing that within the consciousness of Good are all qualities without exception, and knowing that wherever I am is the full expression of Good, I know too that I have complete access to all of the extensive array of Spirit's qualities. This is possible because there is only ONE. I am of that One now and forever.

Today, through this declaration and the power of Life's word, I shake free from my subconscious any ideas or beliefs, whether self-generated or borrowed from the collective, that have distracted me from believing in myself and my ability to be successful, confident, and effective in this world.

Everything I do today, no matter how small the task, I do it with ease and grace, but I do it expertly. Every task, chore or decision I make is made from the consciousness of the I Am.

I access the consciousness that activates in me all the qualities that expand my experience of success and abundance. I am a good decision maker, following through with all things that I commit to, showing up on time, and always completing things expertly. All the skills and talents necessary to support this experience are immediately accessed and downloaded directly from Spirit.

Each day I do something that supports this renewed and awakened idea in me, and as I establish myself as success, I support others in their success, and complete the circle of reciprocity. My generosity further expands my experience of success, and this is good.

For this expansion of consciousness and wonderful demonstration, I am truly grateful to that Creative Stuff that shows up so beautifully.

And so it is!

If you want to be happy, be.
~Leo Tolstoy

*Joy is the way that we experience
our authentic selves;
it is the pure unadulterated
response to Life.
Joy is how we know we
are alive and vital.
Joy is the journey.
Joy is the destination.*
~Michelle Wadleigh

I recognize Spirit in all of its beautiful forms; I know that the depth, the breath, and all of Spirit, are available in, through, and as me. I rest knowing that I can never be separate from Spirit in any way, at any time. On this day, I focus on the JOY that Life is and that I am.

Yes, Spirit is Joy. Spirit is Joy as each human. The beauty and the Joy of Spirit excite and inspire me today and always. Spirit as Joy establishes residence in my mind and body temple.

This Joy has its way with me, and shows up at the most unexpected times. It shows up when I am surrounded by loved ones. but it also shows up in my work and in my alone times. Joy infiltrates my being and activates all good, all healing. and wonderful, beautiful, and inspiring self-expression.

My Joy begins to pour out and spill over, and blesses all people and all situations that I find myself in. I now relate to my Joy in an intimate and completely familiar way. Spirit as Joy is who I am and how I show up in the world.

Every time I smile I exude the Joy that has rooted itself in my consciousness.

Yes, today I am the full expression of Joy. For this and so much more I am grateful.

And so it is!

All illumination, inspiration and realization must come through the self-knowing mind in order to manifest in man.

~Ernest Holmes

There is only One.
One Life.
One vibrant, always available essence of Good.

~Michelle Wadleigh

No time but now.

No place but here.

No outside separate from the inside.

No thought separate from the experience.

No resentment and judgment separate from the pain.

No sin separate from the punishment.

No self-loathing separate from the suffering.

No doubt separate from the fear.

No one but the ONE.

No love separate from the beauty.

No peace separate from the poise.

No demonstration separate from the conviction.

No healing separate from the faith.

No joy separate from being present.

No wisdom separate from being available.

No success separate from working in Principle.

No Private Good—ever. I surrender into the knowing that where I am is the full expression of Spirit.

From the depth of my heart and the knowing of my mind, I accept this as so with gratitude.

And so it is!

My eyes behold the complete and perfect in all Creation,
"In all, overall, and through all." I see the perfect:
There's nothing else to see, and no suggestion of otherness can enter my thought. I know only perfect and the complete.
I am perfect and whole, now.

~Ernest Holmes
The Science of Mind

There is One Life, One Truth and my life is the perfect reflection of this One Life.
I accept all that comes with the All of It with total grace.

~ Michelle Wadleigh

There is One Power, One Presence, One Life, and this One Life is my life now! It is all good, all the time, all around and throughout, and I am grateful to know this and to act from this.

Yes, I am grateful for ALL OF MY LIFE, bar nothing. Every person in my life, every family member and friend are in my life for my life and for its full expression. Each person blesses me because each one is me. I acknowledge that every person in my life, with whom I am in relationship, is an aspect of me and is here to bless me, teach me, and love me.

I bless each and every individual that I have come in contact with, for I know the very presence of each individual in my life is a gift that grows and expands me. I bless them for the obvious gifts they have brought, and for the not-so-obvious gifts. Right now, I declare that I am at peace in the depth of my being, and this peace reflects in each relationship that I have. I am clear about the truth; as within, so without.

So with gratitude for my beautiful and meaningful life, I simply release this word of love and power into Universal Law.

And so it is.

"Courage doesn't always roar.
Sometimes courage is the quiet
voice at the end of the day saying,
"I will try again tomorrow."
~Mary Anne Radmacher

Ready yourself by opening,
by surrendering,
by allowing inspiration to
have its way with you.
~Michelle Wadleigh

There is a place where Spirit resides that is nonlocal, and yet I experience it in my heart and my body temple.

I sense the Allness of Spirit in my soft and quiet moments, and it is these moments that carry and sustain me throughout my day. This is all good and I avail myself now to this complete experience.

I commit and recommit every day to my spiritual practices in order to allow the experience of the One, the Allness, to show up through me in my quiet times and in my busy times.

Making room for Spirit is a declaration of my faith and relationship "in" the One. Regularly returning to a posture of availability indicates my willingness and readiness. And it says, "Use me, love through me, heal through me, and create oneness through me."

Spirit calls. Yes, it whispers, and I listen to the invitation to surrender daily as I return to the practice of listening and surrender, and moment-by-moment, I transcend all limitations of the human condition. I am lifted, loved, and supported. The beauty of my world shows more and more clearly each and every day.

For all that now shows up in my life, I am so grateful, and accept this gift of life in all of its forms.

Thank you to the indwelling Spirit.

And so it is!

*If you know what to do
to reach your goal,
it's not a big enough goal.*
                              ~Bob Proctor

*Live knowing that
something's possible here.
Live from your full
potentiality of Life.
Live life boldly,
without a safety net.*
                              ~Michelle Wadleigh

Today, when I approach anything that *appears* challenging in any way that taxes me, instead of my normal moment of throwing my hands up in the air, today I ask this simple question: *"What's possible here?"* I ask the question, and with absolute conviction, I trust that within record time I will be guided to right solution.

When the *appearance* of stress in one of my relationships shows up, again I remember to ask *"What's possible here?"* and again I trust that right intuition finds me right where I am. The process of healing is quickened because I trust that the Infinite Intelligence that exists will always provide answers and guide me to right solution.

And when I decide to have a bigger experience in my life, and demonstrate in a larger and more fun way, whether it is a new business or a new project or to increase my prosperity, I once again ask, *"What's possible here?"* And with absolute faith in the genius that shows up before me, that I can access at any time, I trust. Yes, I trust all intuition, guidance and impulse to move, act, and make decisions that are in direct alignment with the consciousness that precedes the action.

Asking *"What's Possible Here?"* works because I have already established deep and profound faith in the guiding Principle of Spirit, and trust with all of my being that something greater than my "local self" knows the answers and avails them to me as needed. I begin to live in a faithful, trusting way. I do this each day, with each challenge and every opportunity.

Life is good, and it is always good by means of me. I don't have to know everything because Intelligence does, and since I am all that this Life is, I access this Intelligence in all moments. This is my truth and my practice, and it is good.

And so it is!

*Be the change you wish to see
in the world.*

~Mahatma Ghandi

*Go out of this world,
all used up.
Leave nothing untapped.
Leave nothing unexpressed.*

~ Michelle Wadleigh

As I enter into the fall of this year, this is my prayer:

> May I be gently guided throughout the balance of this year to love generously, deeply, and completely.

> Let me leave my mark on my family and friends and all whom I know, but let this mark be one of love.

> Let me be the carrier of light, the light of Spirit, which is ever present and so healing. And let this healing begin with me.

> Guide me, Spirit, deeper into my soul, and then let me have the courage to trust what I find there.

> May my presence be a present to many, and may that present be welcomed with love and open arms.

> Yes, let me be an uncontaminated vessel through which Spirit may pass and find the open invitation to express.

> For all that is good, pure, and so holy, I am eternally grateful.

> And so it is!

> Amen.

There are only two ways
to live your life. One is as though
nothing is a miracle.
The other is as though
everything is a miracle.

~Albert Einstein

Live believing that all of Life
is working in your favor.
Live in a high expectancy
of good.
Live knowing that you deserve for
life to happen with
ease and grace.
LIVE LIFE FULL OUT!

~Michelle Wadleigh

There is One, only One; this One is who I am at all times, in all ways.

I resonate with all that this One is, and since it is Everything, I am clear that I have access to all good, in all forms, and in great abundance. From every breath that I take to the love that I experience, and to the prosperity that I claim, this One shows up my life in ways expected and unexpected.

I turn away from all distractions immediately, and turn to my desired outcome, immediately placing my attention always on the truth of my being. My truth is, as the One, all good things are possible and available at all times. I have the consciousness to pave the way, and my subconscious aligns with this declaration right now.

I am grateful to know this, and to act from this place. For this good and so much more, I express my gratitude.

And so it is.

Amen.

You only live once, but if you do it right, once is enough.

~Joe Lewis

LIFE IS JUICY, YUMMY
AND DELICIOUS.
Live a life that has you
licking your lips,
laughing out loud,
dancing wildly, and
loving without a safety net.

~Michelle Wadleigh

Oh, Sweet and Powerful Spirit that moves in me, around me, as me in every moment of every day. I am so grateful for the way that Spirit displays its magnificence through me, and I choose to always stand available for It.

This essence that I call Sweet and Powerful lives up to this description all the time. I recognize its sweetness at times when I feel lured to be in my heart, yet I sense its power when I speak my word, and feel the movement of Life itself converging to create that which has been spoken.

I love Spirit in all of its forms and expressions. I love its dependable nature. May I always remain available for all these expressions, each day in every way. Spirit, I declare, have your way through me. I speak my word, and then I trust.

For this grace and this glory, I am so grateful, and I let this be so.

And so it is.

From Rev. Michelle Wadleigh:

Your conscious mind is your gatekeeper. Learning to discipline your attention is time well spent. It will alter the texture and landscape of your life. Pay close attention to your mind, your thinking. Be sure only to collude with that which lifts your life and focuses it in the direction of good, of ease, and of grace.

I hope the following pages will serve as a guide to developing the ability to speak and think in a life affirming way.

You were born with a language inside of you that is recognized by all. Over time, we ceased to remember and use language. It is the language of your heart, your dreams, and your soul. Resurrect your language and speak to all from that place.

~Michelle Wadleigh

Your Heart's Desire

There is a language that we all know how to speak intuitively. It is the language of our hearts, the language of our birthright. Unfortunately, though, through the conditioning of our lives, we have stopped speaking this language or it has become garbled in our heads.

Most of us never learned to answer the question, "What do I really want in my life?" with any degree of power. All too often we get distracted and waylaid on so many levels that it becomes difficult to see through the chaos of our humanity to think about what's possible.

But, when we begin to remember the language of the heart, we remember to think through the Law of Possibility, and in the way of "I deserve" and "I accept." When we recoup this language, and use it to express our hearts' desires, our world begins to take on a different texture, and that texture is so beautiful.

For the new student this sounds unreasonable or Pollyanna-ish, but only in the new mind and only for a short time. This is an understandable reaction because what we teach goes against all of the western human education and conditioning.

For both the new and the more experienced mind, ask yourself if you recall questioning why the wonderment of your child-like way of wishing and wanting without restriction is reserved for the young and for the ones least capable of tangibly creating what they want.

Well, the truth is, it's not.

We teach that there is only One—One Mind, one Power, one Love, one Spirit—One. We believe that we each, to the level of our own acceptance, are the direct offspring of this Intelligent, Creative Nature which is Omnipotent and Omnipresent, and to the degree that we open ourselves to accept our good, it shows up in our lives.

Call it Spirit, Love, Energy or anything you want—but know that It is constantly pouring Itself into and through you, and all that this Eternal and Infinite Source does is morph and change into more good in direct accord with the mold we each provide.

Now we come back to the term, "Your Heart's Desire." If you could speak about all the desires of your heart without restriction, and give full, beautiful descriptive language to the essence of you that lives within your heart, your language would change now and stay changed. If you could really grasp the absolute Truth, told by a millennium of spiritual teachers, that you create as you think and as you speak, you would never again speak a word against yourself or anyone else.

The problem is that you have been taught to disconnect from yourself as a receptive source of power, and in so doing, have become a lazy speaker and thinker which creates a life that does not bring you happiness. **We have nothing but our word and thoughts. We ARE our words and thoughts.**

Are you convinced yet? Remember, the power for transformation is yours and yours alone. The way to activate this power most potently within you is to accept full, 100 per cent responsibility for ALL of your life. The moment you find that willingness, you begin to align yourself with the creative potency of this Universe Law.

Let's assume for now that you are a full-fledged believer; what do you do next?

Listen deeply to your heart, to the depth and purity of your heart, not your ego. As you begin to hear what really matters to you, begin to speak from that creative place. Describe what your heart wants without reservation or resistance or explanation. Allow yourself to find the words that describe what your heart and soul need to feel fully expressed.

For example, if you feel guided to start a new profession and, until now, only your fear and logic have had a voice, quiet your fear by going past it to this deeper listening. Just go directly to what you want and describe it. Don't qualify it or make excuses for why you want it, just allow yourself to be in relationship with the Divine and the flow of good as it moves toward you.

Use healing, descriptive language. Think of a beautiful work of art that uses all color and texture, or a classical piece of music presented by a full orchestra. Be the co-creator of YOU as your own masterpiece. Speak of your life in ways that are loving, healing, creative, and abundant.

Remember, your true heart is wildly passionate with conviction in your favor, and it is highly, highly intelligent. It would not waste time wishing, begging, wanting, and hoping. It only knows acceptance, declaration, and a willingness to Be all that is its birthright.

It uses language that says things like, "I am now willing to accept my good without reservation. I am willing, ready, and open to a life full of joy, peace, harmony, and laughter. Abundance finds me wherever I am because my I am is the I Am of Spirit, one and the same, now and always.

This and things like this are the language of the heart. The heart loves and allows love, which is another way of allowing Spirit to express through you. Speak to Spirit from your heart. Speak with great abandon, passion, and conviction, and then allow your life to unfold in the most beautiful way possible.

May you carry this little reminder with you wherever you go to serve your highest and most beautiful life possible.

A Treatment for You with Love
(Affirmative Prayer)

There is One Life; that Life is the life of Spirit, and it is my life now. All that is good, pure, and holy is the texture of this life that is mine.

From the creative power that this relationship sparks in me, I choose on this day to accept my good and greater good. I choose to accept all love, all power, all prosperity, and perfect health. I feel the surge of Spirit being creative in me and through each and every day, and I call each day good.

All of my mind and heart works harmoniously now as it synchronizes with the creative nature of Spirit, creating through my consciousness with ease and grace. My life is so full and alive because, Spirit as good, is full and alive. I am a vessel for good in my life, the life of my family, my community, and this entire world. I am constantly releasing all thoughts of fear, limitation, and lack as I am always embracing the more of me and the not-yet expressed of me. I celebrate the knowing that all of my life is good and very, very good, including my work, my relationships, and all the activity of my life. Yes, I call it good.

With a deep, profound, and continuously renewing practice of gratitude, I step forth into the acceptance of my good, my grace, accepting Spirit's love like no other. With absolute faith and conviction, I let this word be the creative nature that it is.

And so it is.

Made in the USA
Charleston, SC
11 June 2012